AF413588

This book is dedicated to the memory of my amazing mom, Leta Dallas,
who encouraged me to always continue creating, as well as, my father,
M. Steve Dallas, the wisest and kindest man I have ever known.

This book is also dedicated to my wonderful husband, Bill Vaselopulos,
and our beautiful children, Chris and Alexis, who are
an inspiration to me every day!

This work is inspired by Bosque Eterno de los Niños,
(The Children's Eternal Rainforest, Costa Rica)

Margot Dallas

For my beautiful grandchildren, Ronnie & Zach
With Love, 'Babcia', Barbara

Barbara Kowalska

By Margot Dallas
Illustrated by Barbara Kowalska

There's a place we like to be,

a place of peace,
for you and me,

resting in a sea,
or tree,

a dwelling of tranquility.

This place is home
and when inside...

nestled in
nature,

we can
hide.

A spot to shelter from
the storm,

where there's comfort,
and it's warm.

Earth is a welcome

home for all,

be you ENORMOUS

Pika
15-23 cm/6-8 inches

Monarch Butterfly
7-10 cm/3-4 inches

Bee Hummingbird
6-8 cm/2.4-3.1 inches

Red-eyed Tree Frog
5-7.5 cm/1.5-2.7 inches

Bumblebee
1.5-2 cm/0.6-1 inch

Lightning Bug
5-25 mm/0.5 inch

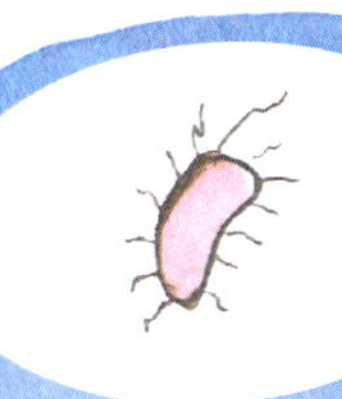

Ladybug
2-10 mm/0.4 inch

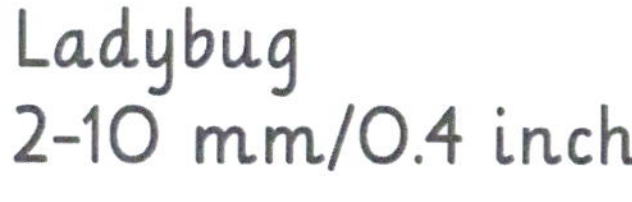

Bioluminescent
Plankton
30um-1 mm

Microscope
40-400 x
magnification

Bacteria
1-10 um
(microns)

Virus
20-200 nm
(nanometers)

All living beings
need a home,

a safe place to return
after they roam.

Colorful quetzals
dwell
in a tree.

Striped dolphins swim in the sea.

Furry bunnies
burrow underground.

Tiny ants, well, they
toil in a mound.

Penguins waddle
across
glistening ice.

For elephants, grassy plains suffice.

Bees buzz busily
inside a hive.

Burrowing in snow,

arctic foxes survive.

Perky pikas call
piles of rocks home.

Fungi
s
w
i
r
l
within churning sea foam.

Red ovenbirds craft nests
of clay and mud.

Tiny caterpillars lodge
within a rose bud.

Mother's pouch warmly
embraces her joey.

Yeast grow in a mixture,
gooey and doughy.

Baby robins snuggle
within a small nest.

Peaceful pandas stretch along
a limb to rest.

All the continents and oceans blue,
provide homes for me and you -

in a tree
or in the sea -

living in tranquility.

HOME

is a place where all can
just BE, surrounded in
LOVE & HARMONY.

THE
END

Thank you profoundly to:
My phenomenally talented artist Barbara,
whose magical illustrations uplifted my words to evoke
a sense of beauty, as they leapt to life across the pages.
My bevy of collaborators who imparted their wisdom, skills,
edits and creativity to help create this work and without
whom I would never have finished this book:
Close friends, Michelle Donofrio and Ronda Kent, who are my editors
extraordinaire and publicists. Also, Casey Dallas, Bill Kashatus,
Rich Becker, Nikki Dallas, Leta Bryan, Rebecca Warga and Lightning Rich.
Thank you to Samantha Click for her beautiful graphic artistry.

Margot Dallas